The Holiday Yule Log Book

Carlo De Vito

CIDER MILL PRESS

BOOK PUBLISHERS

"Happy,

happy Christmas,

that can win us back to the delusions of our childhood days, recall to the old man the pleasures of his youth, and transport the traveler back to his own fireside and quiet home!"–CHARLES DICKENS

"Christmas is not in tinsel and lights and outward show.
The secret lies in an inner glow.
It's lighting a fire inside the heart.
Good will and joy a vital part.
It's higher thought and a greater plan.
It's glorious dream in the soul of man."

—**WILFRED A. PETERSON**, *The Art of Living*

ISBN-13: 978-1-933662-30-5
ISBN-10: 1-933662-30-1

This book may be ordered by mail from the publisher.
Please include $5.00 for postage and handling.
Please support your local bookseller first!

Books published by Cider Mill Press Book Publishers are available at special discounts for bulk purchases in the United States by corporations, institutions, and other organizations. For more information, please contact the publisher.

Cider Mill Press Book Publishers
"Where good books are ready for press"
12 Port Farm Road
Kennebunkport, Maine 04046

Visit us on the web!
www.cidermillpress.com

Design and typography by Joan Sommers Design, Chicago
Printed in China through Imago

1 2 3 4 5 6 7 8 9 0
First Edition

Contents

"The grate

Introduction

had been removed from the wide overwhelming fireplace, to make way for a fire of wood, in the midst of which was an enormous log glowing and blazing, and sending forth a vast volume of light and heat; this I understood was the Yule-log, which the Squire was particular in having brought in and illumined on a Christmas eve, according to ancient custom."

—WASHINGTON IRVING

"The Christmas season stirs up many wonderful memories for each of us. We remember those past celebrations with our friends and families and the special traditions carried on year after year," wrote Carol Morton, Adams County Master Gardener, from Pennsylvania. "There are many Christmas traditions that have gone by the wayside. The burning of the Yule log is a Christmas tradition that has all but died in practice, but the custom lives on in nostalgic images of Christmas past."

The Yule log evokes images of a blazing fire and visions of a house bedecked with Christmas decorations and a giant, green, vibrant jeweled tree brilliantly lit and dominating a room. And of course, those visions would be incomplete without friends and family jamming every corner with good cheer, good food, and much to drink.

These are the holidays. And no holiday setting is ever complete without the concept of the roaring fire, the Yule log, and family, friends, and children singing Christmas carols to brighten the holiday.

The concept of the Yule has truly been lost with time and different authorities disagree with its history and tradition. *Yule* comes from the Norse and was associated with midwinter customs. "Jul" or "Jol" can be interpreted as happy or jolly. But the truth is shrouded in mystery and myth making.

What's not lost on historians is that three writers in particular are responsible for creating the modern version of the holiday season—Charles Dickens, Washington Irving, and Clement C. Moore. Moore wrote the famous "A Visit from St. Nicholas," or better known as "The Night Before Christmas." Moore's contribution is obvious. But more important than the stories themselves, Dickens and Irving created a sense of history about Christmas that was really a blending of fact and fiction. Both authors, in their writings, extolled the virtuous traditions practiced in English homes that led to a revolutionary new approach to Christmas during the Victorian era. This new version of Christmas ultimately became the series of festivities that we know today.

Both writers, in different pieces, wrote of the Yule log as one of those various traditions. And both wrote of caroling. The blazing hearth and the melodic harmonies of the season which have since become entrenched parts of our collective conscious. But what is a Yule log and where does it come from?

The History

Chapter 1

of the Yule Log

"It is Christmas in the mansion,
Yule-log fires and silken frocks;
It is Christmas in the cottage,
Mother's filling little socks.

It is Christmas on the highway,
In the thronging, busy mart;
But the dearest, truest Christmas
Is the Christmas in the heart."

—ANONYMOUS

A Large Consecrated Log

*A*ccording to a pamphlet entitled *Christmas Traditions of France and Canada*, the first tradition of the Yule log held that it be an enormous log, freshly cut, especially selected for the purpose of being the main log of the house for the holiday season. It was meant to be a large log, which would burn through the nights of what was the traditional winter solstice celebration. Other wood and kindling might also be added, but one main log would burn throughout the festivities.

The log would be brought into the house with great ceremony. According to this pamphlet, "On Christmas Eve, the master of the house would place it on the hearth, make libations by sprinkling the trunk with oil, salt and mulled wine and say suitable prayers. In some families, the young girls of the house lit the log with splinters from the preceding year which they had carefully tucked away. In other families, the mother had this privilege. It was said that the cinders of this log could protect the house from lightning and the malevolent powers of the devil. Choices about the variety of wood, the way in which it was lit and the length of time it took to burn constituted a genuine ritual which could vary from region to region."

The beginnings of this tradition come from pagan Scandinavia, where the fire was burnt during the winter solstice as a celebration, the longest night of the year. It signified the turning back of darkness and the welcoming of the lengthening of days and light. It was very similar to the Germanic tradition of burning candles and bringing in evergreens during the same period of the calendar. It was a key holiday in the Scandinavian calendar, and it was they who probably brought the tradition with them to England and Ireland.

Apparently, the custom dated back to the twelfth century. While it was known throughout Europe, it was particularly followed in France and Italy during this period. The Italians referred to the log as a *ceppo*. "This tradition persisted in Quebec as it did in France up until the last quarter of the nineteenth century. Its disappearance coincides with that of great hearths which were gradually replaced by cast-iron stoves. The great log was thus replaced by a smaller one, often embellished with candles and greenery, placed in the center of the table as a Christmas decoration."

"An integral part of Christmas celebrations throughout Feudal Europe, the Yule log came to America directly from England, which inherited the tradition from the pagans of Northern Europe," reports the Pennsylvania Forest Stewardship Program. "There were many regional variations on the ritual, but the English version—the one we know best—was probably the simplest. On Christmas Eve, members of the household ventured into the woods to find and cut a great tree, preferably an oak. Size was important, because the Yule log had to burn throughout the twelve days of Christmas. Once cut, the log was dragged home with much celebration. As many people as possible grabbed onto the ropes to help pull, because doing so was believed to bring good luck in the New Year. Even passersby raised their hats in tribute."

"The Yule-clog is a great log of wood, sometimes the root of a tree, brought into the house with great ceremony, on Christmas eve, laid in the fireplace, and lighted with the brand of last year's clog," wrote Washington Irving. (It's spelled Yule-clog here, but it's just another name for Yule log.) "While it lasted there was great drinking, singing, and telling of tales. Sometimes it was accompanied by Christmas candles, but in the cottages the only light was from the ruddy blaze of the great wood fire. The Yule-clog was to burn all night; if it went out, it was considered a sign of ill luck."

Herrick mentions it in one of his songs:

"Come, bring with a noise
My merrie, merrie boyes,
The Christmas log to the firing:
While my good dame, she
Bids ye all be free,
And drink to your hearts' desiring."

"The Yule-clog is still burnt in many farmhouses and kitchens in England, particularly in the north, and there are several super-stitions connected with it among the peasantry," Irving added. "If a squinting person come to the house while it is burning, or a person barefooted, it is considered an ill omen. The brand remaining from the Yule-clog is carefully put away to light the next year's Christmas fire."

One popular aspect of the Yule log tradition was that no unnecessary work would take place in or around the household as long as the log burned. This season of merriment and reflection was a time for respite from daily labors.

*"Christmas! 'Tis the season for kindling
the fire of hospitality in the hall,
the genial fire of charity in the heart."*

—WASHINGTON IRVING

Start Your Own Tradition

The concept of starting your own Yule log tradition is very easy and fun to do, especially with family and friends.

The first thing you want to do is to find the perfect log. You need to find a log that is well dried out, so that it burns well. If you can, you should think of this sometime during the late summer months, so that by the time the holidays roll around, your log is seasoned, and ready to burn. If not, don't despair. Your log will last a good long time. While oak is preferred, any tree will do.

Next, wrap the log up with evergreen boughs, holly boughs, dried real flowers, and mistletoe and wrap the whole thing up with cloth ribbon. Set the log in your fireplace grate, and add kindling. Dim the lights. You may want to have a family member say something appropriate to the season and your family's beliefs and maybe start off with a carol or two. And then set the kindling ablaze, make sure your screen is correctly and safely in place, and then step back.

Some families take a moment to bid the year adieu, while others also add a moment of silence to consider what changes or events they hope to see happen in the coming year.

A Christmas party is a great time to set ablaze a Yule log and welcome in the new season with wassail and other fun foods of the season.

In olden times, revelers attempted to keep the fire burning for at least twelve hours, symbolizing the course of the calendar year. It was considered bad luck, by some authorities, to disturb the embers during the Christmas Eve meal. Great pains were taken not to touch the fire while any food was still on the holiday table or while anyone was still eating.

Some families related ghost stories during the burning of the fire; others used it as a time to recall past holidays and stories of revelers no longer with them. Often, warmed cider was sipped as the log burned.

If you don't have a working fireplace, you might want to try something different.

Today's traditional Yule log is a centerpiece for the table, adorned with candles, ribbons, and fresh evergreens. It brings the fresh winter greens into the house for the holidays.

● ● ● ● ● ● ● ● ● ● ● ● ● ● ● ● ● ● ●

"I have always thought of Christmas time as a good time;
a kind, forgiving, charitable, pleasant time;
the only time I know of in the long calendar of the year,
when men and women seem by one consent
to open their shut-up hearts freely."

—CHARLES DICKENS

Next Year

After your holiday celebrations have ended and the fireplace has gone completely cold, remember to retain a piece of charred wood from the fire, and store in a safe dry place until the following season. Then you can use it in next year's fire and keep the good cheer of the season going from one year to the next.

According to the Pennsylvania Forest Stewardship Program, "Sometimes Yule log ashes were mixed with livestock feed and spread on the fields to ensure the health of the manor's animals and crops. Uncharred pieces of the log were often made into ceremonial plowshares to guarantee the fertility of the soil."

● ● ● ● ● ● ● ● ● ● ● ● ● ● ● ● ● ● ● ●

"The bûche de Noël *. . . among Francophones on
both sides of the Atlantic it's as much a part of the
Christmas tradition as gingerbread houses are in America.
Think of it as trompe l'oeil baking: If you can paint
a wall to look like marble, why not craft a cake
to look like a hunk of wood ready to burn in the
hearth on Christmas Eve?"*

—KEMP MINIFIE, *Gourmet,* December 2003

Yule Log or Bûche de Noël

oday, the most widely known Yule log is the French-inspired pastry bûche de Noël. The bûche de Noël is usually a sponge cake, or other kind of cake, sometimes vanilla, sometimes chocolate, which is baked in straight sheets, frosted, and then rolled up, and frosted again, with the appearance of a log. The frosting is usually chocolate, to further the idea of it being a log. Many enthusiasts decorate this delicious confection with all manner of things, giving it the further appearance of a log. It is usually decorated with candles and springs of holly and other seasonal touches.

According to urban myths and legends experts Barbara and David P. Mikkelson, traditionally in France, the bûche de Noël was served as the final offering during the Christmas Eve meal. In France, the Christmas Eve meal is called *reveillon*, and usually takes place after the midnight services.

"Time was with most of us, when Christmas Day, encircling all our limited world like a magic ring, left nothing out for us to miss or seek; bound together all our home enjoyments, affections, and hopes; grouped everything and everyone round the Christmas fire, and made the little picture shining in our bright young eyes, complete."

—CHARLES DICKENS

The Televised Yule Log

*T*oday, most people who know about the burning of the Yule log know of the tradition because of the seasonally telecast show on television of the blazing fireplace and holiday carols chiming away in the background. The very first televised Yule Log program occurred in 1966, on station WPIX-TV, channel 11, in New York City. Known simply as "The Yule Log," the show featured a roaring fire and Christmas carols playing in the background. It was televised on Christmas Eve and Christmas Day. It was an immediate hit, so much so that the phenomenon caught on in other cities across the country.

The show featured no live or "on-air" personalities and allowed no commercials during its four-hour run each time it aired. The show was so well loved, WPIX's sister radio station "simulcast" the musical portion of the show for added viewing and listening pleasure, until 1988 when the stations were sold.

WPIX's general manager Fred Thrower is generally credited as the man who invented the television Yule Log. Thrower thought of the idea as a gift to the millions of New Yorkers living in apartments throughout the New York metropolitan region, who lacked traditional fireplaces and thus could not have a warm cozy fire of their own as they celebrated the Yuletide season. Thrower decided to go commercial free, which cost the station a regularly scheduled $4,000 in fees in 1966.

"I thought about all the cave dwellers in New York, all the apartments that don't have fireplaces," he recalled in a 1988 interview. "I thought this might be a wonderful way . . . to let people hear good Christmas carols and to have their own fireplaces burning."

The filming was done at Gracie Mansion, the official residence of the mayor of New York, on the way Upper East Side, earlier in that year. Then mayor John Lindsay approved the filming, and the fire was filmed on 16mm film. Three years later they re-shot the footage at the mayor's residence. In order to gain a better vision point, the fireplace's traditional fire screen was removed. During the filming, a spark shot out and destroyed an antique Persian carpet. According to WPIX staffers, the mayor's office banned WPIX from filming there again. Locations across the country were scouted, and eventually a look-alike fireplace was discovered in Palo Alto, California. They filmed the scene on a hot summer's day, and that film was used at WPIX and other stations across the country for another two decades.

"The Yule Log" premiered on Saturday, December 24, 1966 at 9:30 PM on WPIX Channel 11 in New York City. The original Yule Log program featured only 17 seconds of the fireplace footage shot, which was looped, with a quick dissolve, which seemed seamless. To viewers, the Yule Log burned bright and beautiful and never needed tending. When the film was eventually re-shot years later, the station used a slightly longer seven-minute loop, which still never had to be tended or cajoled, during the television show's four-hour run.

According to Yule Log expert Joe Malzone, "From 1974 until 1989, a special message by WPIX-TV vice president and general manager Richard N. Hughes usually preceded the program while he was running the station. 'The Yule Log' ran every holiday until it was extinguished by new station management in 1990 due to—what else?—the high costs of running the program without commercial interruptions."

In the meantime, the Yule Log had become an institution icon. The show was mocked and lampooned, most notably by MTV's Beavis and Butthead. On the December 17, 1993 episode, the perpetually delinquent duo watched the Yule Log and agreed Christmas was "cool." In 1999, Fred Thrower, the television show's creator died. It was his wish that the program would survive him. In October of 2000, Malzone led a group of faithful Yule Log fans, and founded a website called "Bring Back the Log." Malzone petitioned station management via the Internet to put "The Yule Log" program back on the air. "This film was gathering dust in a warehouse in New Jersey when Julie O'Neal, the station's program director, found it in a film can that simply read 'FIREPLACE.'"

Following the September 2001 attacks, Betty Ellen Berlino, the new general manager of the station, cited that people wanted "comfort food TV." The video was faithfully restored and the soundtrack digitized, thanks to Malzone and his band of merry Yule Log watchers. According to Malzone, "The program was the most-watched TV program in the metropolitan New York area for Christmas Day of that year, and has been winning its time slot annually since." It was big news, being reported in the national press, and covered by such august bodies as the *New York Times*,

Chicago Tribune, and *Los Angeles Times*. Even NPR's *All Things Considered* aired a small segment about the program.

In 2003, Tribune Broadcasting, parent company of WPIX, announced that in addition to being broadcast in New York City, "The Yule Log" would be broadcast in additional U.S. television markets on other Tribune-owned television stations. The program made its "national" debut in 2004 on WGN-TV and its sibling Superstation. That same year, the program was shown in high-definition television for the very first time. The Yule Log now found its way into more than 65 million homes.

The original television show spawned an entire mini-industry. It seems every region has its share in the claim of a beloved Yule Log. "What would a Northwest Christmas Eve be without the ol' yule log?" wrote Pete Schulberg, the host of "Portland's Morning News" on Oregon's KPAM (AM). "I'm not talking about just any Yule log, mind you: I'm referring to the traditional KOPB (10) special, 'Yule Log.' It's the consummate reality show: a log burning. This 20-year TV tradition drives home the point that you're watching what is unarguably the most boring—but somehow soothing—program of the year." Recent version's of Portland's famed Yule Log have featured updated soundtracks including such contemporary groups as Barenaked Ladies, Boyz II Men, and other favorites.

Canada alone had several versions of the Yule Log, which aired across the country. Rhiannon Coppin of British Columbia,

Canada, recalled her family all sitting together in the festively decorated living room. They had eaten and were sated and seated. "The usual once-a-year conversations faded into an uncomfortable lull. Suddenly, a beacon from beyond appeared, uniting my family at once as we began screeching an excited, shared refrain: 'The hand! The hand!'" wrote Rhiannon for *Seven Oaks* magazine.

"Our prompt was a bejewelled crone's hand that, reaching out from the side of our television set, placed a fresh log on the SHAW cable community channel's broadcast of The Burning Log. The new piece of wood signaled the start of another loop of the tape that brought the convenience and charm of a brightness-adjustable, child-safe, scentless fire to countless Lower Mainland families and pyromaniacs alike. . . . My family stared, transfixed, as the wood blackened and melted away, the logs slowly collapsing onto one another." Other televised Yule Logs were sponsored, it seems by gas companies, and their video was a blazing, roaring gas fireplace.

The CHUM Television group in Canada borrowed the concept and began to run its version of "The Yule Log" on its stations in 2004.

In 2005, Tribune Broadcasting began making a version of the Yule Log video recorded in MPEG-4 format available for download, advertising it as a "Portable Yule Log" for those traveling during the holiday season.

Poems to Read

Chapter 2

'round the Yule Log

The Yule Log

Come, bring with a noise,
My merry, merry boys,
The Christmas log to the firing;
While my good dame, she
Bids ye all be free,
And drink to your heart's desiring.

With the last year's brand
Light the new block, and
For good success in his spending,
On your Psaltries play,
That sweet luck may
Come while the log is tending.

ROBERT HERRICK

Welcome Yule

Welcome be thou, heavenly King,
Welcome born on this morning,
Welcome for whom we shall sing,
Welcome Yule,

Welcome be ye Stephen and John,
Welcome Innocents every one,
Welcome Thomas Martyr one,
Welcome Yule.

Welcome be ye, good New Year,
Welcome Twelfth Day, both in fere,
Welcome saints, loved and dear,
Welcome Yule.

Welcome be ye, Candlemas,
Welcome be ye, Queen of Bliss,
Welcome both to more and less,
Welcome Yule.

Welcome be ye that are here,
Welcome all, and make good cheer,
Welcome all, another year,
Welcome Yule.

SLOANE MANUSCRIPTS, MEDIEVAL MANUSCRIPTS

Yule Log (1889)

Come gather round the Yule log's blaze!
In light and laughter leap the flames,
The fire sings like a hymn of praise,
Its warmth the heart of winter tames.

Behold the house is all aglow
From door to roof with Christmas cheer!
What matter how the cold winds blow!
Comfort and peace and joy are here.

Come share the Yule log's glorious heat!
For many a year the grand old tree
Stood garnering up the sunshine sweet,
To keep for our festivity.

And now our Christmas Eve to bless
See how it yields its ardent rays!
As if to wish you happiness,
Honor and love and length of days.

"Welcome," it smiles with every beam,
saluting you with kindly power.
Its golden banners flash and gleam,
Its mellow splendor crowns the hour.

Then gather round the flames so bright,
Forget that winter blasts are stern,
So fervently this holy night
On friendships' hearth the Yule fires burn.

CELIA LAIGHTON THAXTER

A Visit from St. Nicholas
[The Night Before Christmas]

Twas the night before Christmas, when all through the house
Not a creature was stirring, not even a mouse;
The stockings were hung by the chimney with care,
In hopes that St. Nicholas soon would be there;
The children were nestled all snug in their beds,
While visions of sugar-plums danced in their heads;
And mamma in her kerchief, and I in my cap,
Had just settled our brains for a long winter's nap—
When out on the lawn there arose such a clatter,
I sprang from my bed to see what was the matter,
Away to the window I flew like a flash,
Tore open the shutters and threw up the sash.
The moon, on the breast of the new-fallen snow,
Gave a lustre of mid-day to objects below;
When, what to my wondering eyes should appear,

But a miniature sleigh, and eight tiny rein-deer,
With a little old driver, so lively and quick,
I knew in a moment it must be St. Nick.
More rapid than eagles his coursers they came,
And he whistled, and shouted, and called them by name;
"Now, Dasher! now, Dancer! now, Prancer and Vixen!
On! Comet, on! Cupid, on! Dunder and Blitzen—
To the top of the porch, to the top of the wall!
Now, dash away, dash away, dash away all!"
As dry leaves that before the wild hurricane fly,
When they meet with an obstacle, mount to the sky,
So, up to the house-top the coursers they flew,
With a sleigh full of toys—and St. Nicholas too.
And then in a twinkling I heard on the roof,
The prancing and pawing of each little hoof.
As I drew in my head, and was turning around,
Down the chimney St. Nicholas came with a bound.
He was dressed all in fur from his head to his foot,
And his clothes were all tarnished with ashes and soot;
A bundle of toys he had flung on his back,
And he looked like a peddler just opening his pack;
His eyes, how they twinkled! his dimples how merry!
His cheeks were like roses, his nose like a cherry,
His droll little mouth was drawn up like a bow,

And the beard on his chin was as white as the snow;
The stump of a pipe he held tight in his teeth,
And the smoke, it encircled his head like a wreath.
He had a broad face, and a little round belly
That shook when he laughed, like a bowl full of jelly.
He was chubby and plump—a right jolly old elf;
And I laughed when I saw him in spite of myself.
A wink of his eye, and a twist of his head,
Soon gave me to know I had nothing to dread.
He spoke not a word, but went straight to his work,
And filled all the stockings; then turned with a jerk,
And laying his finger aside of his nose,
And giving a nod, up the chimney he rose.
He sprang to his sleigh, to his team gave a whistle,
And away they all flew like the down of a thistle;
But I heard him exclaim, ere he drove out of sight,

"MERRY CHRISTMAS TO ALL, AND TO ALL A GOOD NIGHT!"

CLEMENT C. MOORE

The Magick and Myth

Chapter 3

ology of the Yule Log

The History of the Spiritual Side of the Yule Log

The Yule log is seen as central to the holiday festivities. But some cite a more spiritual association. According to the Mikkelsons, "The log is kindled from the remains of the previous year's Yule fire." The idea was that the partially burnt piece of the fire held magical properties that kept more malevolent spirits at bay and was a good omen to keep around your home throughout the year. The piece was then used to start the next Christmas fire a year later, thus keeping the season's magic going. "The Yule log symbolizes the light returning to conquer the darkness. According to tradition, the log must either have been harvested from the householder's land, or given as a gift . . . it must never have been bought. Once dragged into the house and placed in the fireplace it was decorated in seasonal greenery, doused with cider or ale, and dusted with flour before set ablaze. The log would burn throughout the night, then smolder for 12 days after before being ceremonially put out."

More often than not, today's modern Yule log is seen as a small log, which holds three candles. It is also adorned with holiday greenery and used as a centerpiece.

Yule Log Magick

According to the Mikkelsons, "The Yule Log is a remnant of the bonfires that the European pagans would set ablaze at the time of winter solstice. These bonfires symbolized the return of the Sun."

To emulate the days of old in your own fireplace, you want a large log that fits safely into your firebox. Decorate the log with pine cones, dried holly, some burnable ribbons, and some dried kindling.

The Mikkelsons report that your Yule log can be made of any wood, but oak is the traditional choice. However, they point out that each different wood releases its own kind of magic according to history and tradition:

Ash—brings protection, prosperity, and health

Aspen—invokes understanding of the grand design

Birch—signifies new beginnings

Holly—inspires visions and reveals past lives

Oak—brings healing, strength, and wisdom

Pine—signifies prosperity and growth

Willow—invokes the Goddess to achieve desires

Celtic Mythology

*O*f course, there is a bit of the pagan world in the concept of the Yule log. According to mythology expert Terri Paajanen, the Holly King and the Oak King are part of Celtic mythology, who fight for power every year at Yule and Midsummer. The Celtic Druids believed that the Holly King and the Oak King battled "twice a year, once at Yule and once at Midsummer (Litha) to see who would rule over the next half of the year. At Yule, the Oak King wins and at Litha, the Holly King is victorious. In other words, the Oak King rules over the lighter half of the year, and the Holly King over the darker half. The change from one to the other is a common theme for rituals at Yule, and also at Midsummer."

Paajanen also cites another version of the pagan myth, where the two "do not directly switch places twice a year, but rather both live simultaneously. The Oak King is born at Yule, and his strength grows through the spring . . . and then . . . the Holly King lives a reverse existence, and is born at Midsummer." The idea was that each king symbolized the natural and spiritual aspects of man. "The time of the Oak King is for growth, development, healing, and new projects. The Holly King's time is for rest, reflection, and learning."

Classic

Chapter 4

Christmas Recipes

Classic Yule Log or Bûche de Noël

For the cake:
½ cup sifted cake flour
¼ cup unsweetened cocoa powder
1 teaspoon baking powder
¼ teaspoon salt
½ cup sugar
3 eggs, separated
¼ cup milk

For the frosting:
2 cups heavy whipping cream
8 (1-ounce) squares semisweet chocolate, melted
¼ cup butter, softened
⅛ cup confectioners' sugar

For cake assembly:
⅛ cup confectioners' sugar
1½ cups whipped cream
½ teaspoon green food coloring
8 ounces marzipan
cinnamon candies, snowmen

Preheat oven to 350°F (175°C).

1. Grease a 15 x 10-inch jelly-roll pan. Line with waxed paper.

2. Grease paper.

3. Sift together flour, cocoa, baking powder, and salt.

4. Beat together sugar and egg yolks at high speed until light and fluffy. At low speed, alternately beat milk and flour mixture into egg mixture.

5. Using clean beaters, beat egg whites at high speed until stiff, but not dry, so that peaks form.

6. Fold one third of beaten whites into batter. Fold in remaining whites. Spread batter in prepared pan; smooth top.

7. Bake cake at 350°F (175°C) until set, 12 minutes.

8. Dust a clean cloth with confectioners' sugar. Turn cake out onto prepared cloth. Remove waxed paper. Trim cake edges.

9. Starting with a long side, roll up cake, jelly-roll style. Transfer, seam-side down, to a wire rack to cool for 30 minutes.

10. Unroll cake; remove cloth. Spread whipped cream over cake up to 1 inch of edges. Re-roll cake. Place seam-side down on serving plate.

11. To prepare frosting, in a small saucepan, bring heavy cream,

melted chocolate, and butter to a boil over medium heat, stirring vigorously until blended. Remove from heat. Let stand until set. Spread frosting over top and sides of cake.

12. To prepare garnish, dust work surface with confectioners' sugar. Knead food coloring into marzipan until blended. Using a rolling pin dusted with confectioners' sugar, roll marzipan to a ⅛-inch thickness. Using a small knife, cut out leaves. Arrange leaves, cinnamon candies, and snowmen on top of cake and around plate. Dust with confectioners' sugar. Enjoy!

Serves 10

Eggnog

Make sure to have a whisk or high-speed mixer to beat your egg whites as fluffy as possible. Remember, as you prepare your eggnog, you should do everything possible to ensure its fluffiness. Slowness counts.

For a non-alcoholic version of this recipe, omit the whiskey and rum and substitute an additional 1 ½ cups whole milk

> 8 fresh eggs (separated into yolks/whites)
> 1 cup sugar
> 1 cup dark rum
> 3 cups whole milk
> 2 ½ cups whiskey
> 2 cups heavy/whipping cream
> ground cinnamon and nutmeg

1. Separate eggs.
2. Beat egg-yolks with one-half cup of sugar, set aside.
3. Beat egg-whites until stiff.
4. Mix remaining sugar with the egg whites.
5. Fold the yolks into the whites.
6. Fold in rum.
7. Fold in milk.
8. Fold in whiskey.

9. Fold in ½ of cream.
10. Whip rest of cream and fold in.

Alcoholic version serves 12–14
Non-alcoholic version serves 8–10

Gingerbread

6 cups all-purpose flour
1¾ cups sugar
⅔ cup shortening
1 tablespoon ground cinnamon
1 tablespoon ground ginger
2 teaspoons baking powder
1¼ teaspoons salt
1 teaspoon baking soda
1 teaspoon vanilla extract
1 8-oz. container sour cream
2 eggs

1. In a large bowl, add 3½ cups flour and all other ingredients.
2. At low speed, with mixer, beat until well mixed. When well blended, begin to slowly knead in remaining flour until well mixed. Should make a soft dough. Craft into two or three balls and wrap each in plastic wrap. Refrigerate 2½ hours.

3. When read to bake, preheat oven to 350°F.

4. Lightly flour work surface. Take balls out of refrigerator. Knead in small amount of flour and work dough until smooth.

5. Place dough on cookie sheet. With rolling pin, roll out until you reach desired thickness. Some people like thick gingerbread dough, others like it paper thin. Roll to your own liking. Make sure to constantly flour your rolling pin for best results.

6. If you prefer, you can roll out the dough on your counter, with a coating of flour, and cut into desired shapes.

7. Bake until golden brown or when very firm to the touch.

8. Remove cookie sheet from oven and cool on wire rack 5 minutes.

Serves 6–8

Wassail

Wassail is a traditional holiday winter-warmer, a drink that dates back to the Middle Ages. Some versions are made with ale or beer and others are made with wine. In this recipe, you can make it with either.

4 roasted apples
6 cups ale or wine
1 cup sugar
pinch of ground cloves
pinch of ground nutmeg
pinch of ground cinnamon
pinch of ground ginger
6 eggs, beaten

1. Bake four cored apples with a dash of cinnamon in an oven for 1 hour at 300°F.
2. Pour ale in a saucepan and heat on low heat.
3. Add sugar and spices and bring to a boil.
4. Remove from heat.
5. In a separate bowl, beat the eggs.
6. Slowly add a small amount of the hot mixture to the beaten eggs.
7. Return saucepan to stove and cook, stirring constantly, until slightly thickened. Add the remainder of the egg mixture to the pan.
8. Place apples and hot mixture in a punch bowl and serve.

A non-alcoholic version can be made substituting apple juice or a mixture of half apple juice and half cranberry.

Serves 12–14

Chapter 5

Holiday Lyrics

Adeste, Fideles (O Come, All Ye Faithful)

Words and Music by John Francis Wade

1. Adeste, fideles,
   Laeti, triumphantes,
   Venite, venite in Bethlehem!
   Natum videte
   Regem Angelorum!

Refrain Venite, adoremus!
Venite, adoremus!
Venite adoremus Dominum!

2. Cantet nunc "Io!"
   Chorus angelorum;
   Cantet nunc aula caelestium:
   "Gloria in excelsis Deo!"
   Refrain

3. Ergo qui natus,
   Die hodierna
   Jesu, tibi sit gloria,
   Patris aeterni Verbum caro factum.
   Refrain

Angels We Have Heard on High

Traditional French Carol
Translated by James Chadwick

1. Angels we have heard on high
   Sweetly singing o'er the plains,
   And the mountains in reply
   Echoing their joyous strains.

Refrain Gloria in excelsis Deo,
Gloria in excelsis Deo.

2. Shepherds, why this jubilee?
   Why your joyous strains prolong?
   What the gladsome tidings be
   Which inspire your heav'nly song?
   Refrain

Away in a Manger

Words by John T. McFarland (verse 3)
Music by William J. Kirkpatrick

1. Away in a manger, No crib for a bed,
   The little Lord Jesus laid down His sweet head.
   The stars in the sky looked down where He lay,
   The little Lord Jesus asleep on the hay.

2. The cattle are lowing, the Baby awakes
   But little Lord Jesus, no crying He makes.
   I love Thee, Lord Jesus, look down from the sky,
   And stay by my side, until morning is nigh.

3. Be near me, Lord Jesus; I ask Thee to stay
   Close by me forever and love me, I pray.
   Bless all the dear children in Thy tender care,
   And fit us for heaven to love with Thee there.

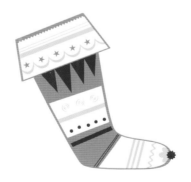

Deck the Hall

Traditional Welsh Carol

1. Deck the hall with boughs of holly,
   fa la la la la, la la la la.
   Tis the season to be jolly,
   fa la la la la, la la la la.
   Don we now our gay apparel,
   fa la la la la, la la la la.
   Troll the ancient Yuletide carol.
   Fa la la la la, la la la la.

2. See the blazing yule before us,
   fa la la la la, la la la la.
   Strike the harp and join the chorus,
   fa la la la la, la la la la.
   Follow me in merry measure,
   fa la la la la, la la la la.
   While I tell of Yuletide treasure.
   Fa la la la la, la la la la.

3. Fast away the old year passes,
   fa la la la la, la la la la.
   Hail the new, ye lads and lasses,
   fa la la la la, la la la la.
   Sing we joyous all together,
   fa la la la la, la la la la.

Heedless of the wind and weather.
Fa la la la la, la la la la.

The First Noël

17th Century English Carol
Music from W. Sandys' Christmas Carols

1. The first noël the angel did say
   Was to certain poor shepherds in fields as they lay;
   In fields where they lay keeping their sheep,
   On a cold winter's night that was so deep.

Refrain Noël, Noël, Noël, Noël,
   Born is the King of Israel.

2. They looked up and saw a star
   Shining in the East, beyond them far.
   And to the earth it gave great light,
   And so it continued both day and night.
   Refrain

3. And by the light of that same star,
   Three wise men came from country far.
   To seek for a King was their intent,
   And to follow the star wherever it went.
   Refrain

4. This star drew nigh to the northwest;
   O'er Bethlehem it took its rest.
   And there it did both stop and stay,
   Right o'er the place where Jesus lay.
   Refrain

5. Then entered in those wise men three
   Full rev'rently upon their knee;
   And offered there in His presence,
   Their gold and myrrh and frankincense.
   Refrain

6. Then let us all with one accord
   Sing praises to our heav'nly Lord,
   That hath made heav'n and earth of nought,
   And with His blood mankind hath bought.
   Refrain

God Rest Ye Merry, Gentlemen

Traditional

1. God rest you merry, gentlemen,
   Let nothing you dismay.
   Remember Christ our Savior
   Was born on Christmas Day,
   To save us all from Satan's pow'r
   When we were gone astray.

Refrain O tidings of comfort and joy,
Comfort and joy,
O tidings of comfort and joy.

2. From God our Heav'nly Father
A blessed angel came,
And unto certain shepherds
Brought tidings to the same,
How that in Bethlehem was born
The Son of God by name.
Refrain

3. In Bethlehem, in Jewry
This blessed Babe was born,
And laid within a manger
Upon this holy morn,
The which his Mother Mary
Did nothing take in scorn.
Refrain

4. "Fear not then," said the Angel,
"Let nothing you affright,
This day is born a Savior
Of a pure Virgin bright,
To free all those who trust in Him
From Satan's power and might."
Refrain

5. The shepherds at those tidings
   Rejoiced much in mind,
   And left their flocks a-feeding,
   In tempest, storm, and wind:
   And went to Bethlehem straightway,
   The Song of God to find.
   Refrain

6. And when they came to Bethlehem
   Where our dear Savior lay,
   They found Him in a manger,
   Where oxen feed on hay;
   His Mother Mary kneeling down,
   Unto the Lord did pray.
   Refrain

7. Now to the Lord sing praises,
   All you within this place,
   And with true love and brotherhood
   Each other now embrace;
   This holy tide of Christmas
   All other doth deface.
   Refrain

Good King Wenceslas

Words by John M. Neale
Traditional Melody

1. Good King Wenceslas looked out
   On the feast of Stephen,
   When the snow lay 'round about,
   Deep and crisp and even.
   Brightly shone the moon that night,
   Though the frost was cruel.
   When a poor man came in sight,
   Gath'ring winter fuel.

2. "Hither, page, and stand by me,
   If though know'st it, telling,
   Yonder peasant, who is he?
   Where and what his dwelling?"
   "Sire, he lives a good league hence,
   Underneath the mountain;
   Right against the forest fence,
   By Saint Agnes's fountain."

3. "Bring me flesh, and bring me wine,
   Bring me pine-logs hither;
   Thou and I will see him dine,
   When we bear them thither."
   Page and monarch, forth they went,

Forth they went together;
Through the rude wind's wild lament:
And the bitter weather.

4. "Sire, the night is darker now,
And the wind blows stronger;
Fails my heart, I know not how,
I can go not longer."
"Mark my footsteps, my good page,
Tread thou in them boldly:
Thou shalt find the winter's rage
Freeze thy blood less coldly."

5. In his master's steps he trod,
Where the snow lay dinted;
Heat was in the very sod
Which the saint had printed.
Therefore, Christian men, be sure,
Wealth or rank possessing,
Ye who now will bless the poor,
Shall yourselves find blessing.

Hark! The Herald Angels Sing

Words by Charles Wesley, altered by George Whitefield
Music by Felix Mendelssohn-Bartholdy
Arranged by William H. Cummings

1. Hark! The herald angels sing,
   "Glory to the newborn King!
   Peace on earth, and mercy mild,
   God and sinners reconciled."
   Joyful all ye nations rise,
   Join the triumph of the skies;
   With th'angelic host proclaim,
   "Christ is born in Bethlehem."

Refrain Hark! The herald angels sing,
   "Glory to the newborn King!"

2. Christ, by highest heav'n adored,
   Christ, the everlasting Lord;
   Late in time behold him come,
   Offspring of the virgin's womb.
   Veiled in flesh the Godhead see;
   Hail th'Incarnate Deity,
   Pleased as Man with men to dwell,
   Jesus our Emmanuel!
   Refrain

3. Hail, the heav'nborn Prince of Peace!
   Hail, the Sun of Righteousness!
   Light and life to all He brings,
   Ris'n with healing in His wings.
   Mild He lays His glory by,
   Born that man no more may die,
   Born to raise the sons of earth,
   Born to give them second birth.
   Refrain

The Holly and the Ivy

Traditional

1. The holly and the ivy,
   When they are both full grown,
   Of all the trees that are in the wood,
   The holly bears the crown.

Refrain The rising of the sun
   And the running of the deer,
   The playing of the merry organ,
   Sweet singing in the choir.

2. The holly bears a blossom,
   As white as lily flow'r,
   And Mary bore sweet Jesus Christ,

To be our sweet Savior.
Refrain

3. The holly bears a berry,
   As red as any blood,
   And Mary bore sweet Jesus Christ,
   To do poor sinners good.
   Refrain

It Came Upon the Midnight Clear

Words by Edmund Hamilton Sears
Music by Richard Storrs Willis

1. It came upon the midnight clear,
   That glorious song of old,
   From angels bending near the earth
   To touch their harps of gold.
   "Peace on the earth, good will to men,
   From heaven's all gracious King."
   The world in solemn stillness lay
   To hear the angels sing.

2. Still through the cloven skies they come
   With peaceful wings unfurled.
   And still their heavenly music floats
   O'er all the weary world;

61

Above its sad and lowly plains
They bend on hovering wing
And ever over its Babel sounds
The blessed angels sing.

3. And ye beneath life's crushing load,
   Whose forms are bending low,
   Who toil along the climbing way
   With painful steps and slow,
   Look now! for glad and golden hours
   Come swiftly on the wing.
   O rest beside the weary road
   And hear the angels sing.

4. For, lo, the days are hast'ning on,
   By prophet bards foretold,
   When with the ever circling years
   Comes round the age of gold,
   When peace shall over all the earth
   Its ancient splendor fling,
   And the whole world give back the song
   Which now the angels sing.

Jingle Bells

Words and Music by J. Pierpont

1. Dashing through the snow
   in a one-horse open sleigh,
   o'er the fields we go,
   laughing all the way.
   Bells on bob-tail ring,
   making spirits bright;
   what fun it is to ride and sing
   a sleighing song tonight! Oh!

Refrain Jingle bells, jingle bells,
jingle all the way.
Oh, what fun it is to ride
in a one-horse open sleigh! Hey!
Jingle bells, jingle bells,
jingle all the way.
Oh, what fun it is to ride
in a one-horse open sleigh.

2. A day or two ago
   I thought I'd take a ride,
   and soon Miss Fanny Bright
   was seated by my side.
   The horse was lean and lank,
   misfortune seemed his lot;

he got into a drifted bank
and we, we got upsot. Oh!
Refrain

3. Now the ground is white;
    go it while you're young.
    Take the girls tonight
    and sing this sleighing song.
    Just get a bob-tailed bay,
    two-forty for his speed,
    then hitch him to an open sleigh
    and crack! you'll take the lead! Oh!
    Refrain

Jolly Old St. Nicholas

Traditional 19th Century American Carol

1. Jolly old Saint Nicholas,
    Lean your ear this way.
    Don't you tell a single soul
    What I'm going to say;
    Christmas Eve is coming soon,
    Now, you dear old man
    Whisper what you'll bring to me;
    Tell me if you can.

2. When the clock is striking twelve,
   When I'm fast asleep,
   Down the chimney broad and black,
   With your pack you'll creep;
   All the stockings you will find
   Hanging in a row.
   Mine will be the shortest one,
   You'll be sure to know.

3. Johnny wants a pair of skates;
   Susy wants a sled;
   Nellie wants a picture book,
   Yellow, blue, and red.
   Now I think I'll leave to you
   What to give the rest:
   Choose for me, dear Santa Claus,
   You will know the best.

Joy to the World

Words by Isaac Watts
Music by George Frideric Handel

1. Joy to the world! The Lord is come;
   Let earth receive her King;
   Let ev'ry heart prepare Him room,
   And heav'n and nature sing,
   And heav'n and nature sing,
   And heav'n, and heav'n, and nature sing.

2. Joy to the earth! The Savior reigns;
   Let men their songs employ;
   While fields and floods, rocks, hills and plains
   Repeat the sounding joy,
   Repeat the sounding joy,
   Repeat, repeat, the sounding joy.

3. He rules the world with truth and grace,
   And makes the nations prove
   The glories of His righteousness
   And wonders of His love,
   And wonders of His love,
   And wonders, wonders, of His love.

O Christmas Tree

Traditional German Carol

1. O Christmas tree! O Christmas tree,
   you stand in verdant beauty!
   O Christmas tree, O Christmas tree,
   you stand in verdant beauty!
   Your boughs are green in summer's glow,
   and do not fade in winter's snow.
   O Christmas tree, O Christmas tree,
   you stand in verdant beauty!

2. O Christmas tree! O Christmas tree,
   much pleasure doth thou bring me!
   O Christmas tree, O Christmas tree,
   much pleasure doth thou bring me!
   For ev'ry year the Christmas tree
   brings to us all both joy and glee.
   O Christmas tree, O Christmas tree,
   much pleasure doth thou bring me!

3. O Christmas tree! O Christmas tree,
   thy candles shine out brightly!
   O Christmas tree, O Christmas tree,
   thy candles shine out brightly!

Each bough doth hold its tiny light
that makes each toy to sparkle bright.
O Christmas tree, O Christmas tree,
thy candles shine out brightly!

O Come, All Ye Faithful (Adeste, Fideles)

Words and Music by John Francis Wade
Latin Words Translated by Frederick Oakeley

1. O come, all ye faithful, joyful and triumphant,
   O come ye, O come ye to Bethlehem.
   Come and behold Him, born the King of angels.

Refrain O come, let us adore Him,
   O come, let us adore Him,
   O come, let us adore Him,
   Christ, the Lord!

2. Sing, choirs of angels, sing in exultation,
   O sing all ye citizens of heav'n above.
   Glory to God in the highest.
   Refrain

3. Yea, Lord, we greet Thee, born this happy morning,
   Jesus, to Thee be all glory giv'n.
   Word of the Father, now in flesh appearing.
   Refrain

O Little Town of Bethlehem

Words by Phillips Brooks
Music by Lewis H. Redner

1. O little town of Bethlehem,
   How still we see thee lie!
   Above thy deep and dreamless sleep
   The silent stars go by.
   Yet in thy dark streets shineth
   The everlasting light.
   The hopes and fears of all the years
   Are met in thee tonight.

2. Christ is born of Mary,
   And gathered all above,
   While mortals sleep the angels keep
   Their watch of wond'ring love.
   O morning stars, together
   Proclaim the holy birth!
   And praises sing to God the King,
   And peace to men on earth!

Silent Night

Words by Joseph Mohr
Translated by John F. Young
Music by Franz X. Gruber

1. Silent night, holy night,
   All is calm, all is bright.
   Round yon virgin Mother and Child.
   Holy Infant so tender and mild.
   Sleep in heavenly peace,
   Sleep in heavenly peace.

2. Silent night, holy night,
   Shepherds quake at the sight.
   Glories stream from heaven afar,
   Heav'nly hosts sing Alleluia,
   Christ the Savior is born!
   Christ the Savior is born!

3. Silent night, holy night,
   Son of God, love's pure light,
   Radiant beams from Thy holy face,
   With the dawn of redeeming grace,
   Jesus, Lord, at Thy birth.
   Jesus, Lord, at Thy birth.

The Twelve Days of Christmas

Traditional English Carol

1. On the first day of Christmas,
   my true love sent to me,
   a partridge in a pear tree.

2. On the second day of Christmas,
   my true love sent to me,
   two turtle doves
   and a partridge in a pear tree.

3. On the third day of Christmas,
   my true love sent to me,
   three French hens,
   two turtle doves,
   and a partridge in a pear tree.

4. On the fourth day of Christmas,
   my true love sent to me,
   four calling birds,
   three French hens,
   two turtle doves,
   and a partridge in a pear tree.

5. On the fifth day of Christmas,
   my true love sent to me,
   five golden rings,

four calling birds,
three French hens,
two turtle doves,
and a partridge in a pear tree.

6. On the sixth day of Christmas,
my true love sent to me,
six geese a-laying,
five golden rings,
four calling birds,
three French hens,
two turtle doves,
and a partridge in a pear tree.

7. On the seventh day of Christmas,
my true love sent to me,
seven swans a-swimming,
six geese a-laying,
five golden rings,
four calling birds,
three French hens,
two turtle doves,
and a partridge in a pear tree.

8. On the eighth day of Christmas,
my true love sent to me,
eight maids a-milking,
seven swans a-swimming,

six geese a-laying,
five golden rings,
four calling birds,
three French hens,
two turtle doves,
and a partridge in a pear tree.

9. On the ninth day of Christmas,
my true love sent to me,
nine ladies dancing,
eight maids a-milking,
seven swans a-swimming,
six geese a-laying,
five golden rings,
four calling birds,
three French hens,
two turtle doves,
and a partridge in a pear tree.

10. On the tenth day of Christmas,
my true love sent to me,
ten lords a-leaping,
nine ladies dancing,
eight maids a-milking,
seven swans a-swimming,
six geese a-laying,
five golden rings,
four calling birds,

three French hens,
two turtle doves,
and a partridge in a pear tree.

11. On the eleventh day of Christmas,
my true love sent to me,
eleven pipers piping,
ten lords a-leaping,
nine ladies dancing,
eight maids a-milking,
seven swans a-swimming,
six geese a-laying,
five golden rings,
four calling birds,
three French hens,
two turtle doves,
and a partridge in a pear tree.

12. On the twelfth day of Christmas,
my true love sent to me,
twelve drummers drumming,
eleven pipers piping,
ten lords a-leaping,
nine ladies dancing,
eight maids a-milking,
seven swans a-swimming,
six geese a-laying,
five golden rings,

74

four calling birds,
three French hens,
two turtle doves,
and a partridge in a pear tree.

Up on the Housetop

Words and Music by B. R. Handy

Up on the housetop reindeer pause,
Out jumps good old Santa Claus;
Down thru the chimney with lots of toys,
All for the little ones, Christmas joys.

Refrain Ho, ho, ho!
Who wouldn't go!
Ho, ho, ho!
Who wouldn't go!
Up on the housetop,
Click, click, click
Down thru the chimney with
Good Saint Nick.

2. First comes the stocking of little Nell;
Oh, dear Santa, fill it well;
Give her a dollie that laughs and cries,
One that will open and shut her eyes.
Refrain

We Three Kings of Orient Are

Words and Music by John H. Hopkins, Jr.

We three kings of Orient are;
Bearing gifts we traverse afar,
Field and fountain, moor and mountain,
Following yonder star.

Refrain   O star of wonder, star of night,
Star with royal beauty bright,
Westward leading, still proceeding,
Guide us to thy perfect light.

We Wish You a Merry Christmas

Traditional English Carol

1. We wish you a Merry Christmas,
We wish you a Merry Christmas,
We wish you a Merry Christmas
And a happy New Year.

Refrain   Good tidings we bring to you and your kin,
Good tidings for Christmas and a happy New Year.

2. Please bring us a figgy pudding,
   Please bring us a figgy pudding,
   Please bring us a figgy pudding
   And a cup of good cheer.
   Refrain

3. We like figgy figgy pudding,
   We like figgy figgy pudding,
   We like figgy figgy pudding
   And a cup of good cheer.
   Refrain

4. We won't go until we've got some,
   We won't go until we've got some,
   We won't go until we've got some,
   Kindly bring some out here.
   We wish you a Merry Christmas
   And a happy New Year.
   Refrain

What Child Is This?

Words by William C. Dix
Based on "Greensleeves"
Old English Air

1. What Child is this, who, laid to rest,
   On Mary's lap is sleeping?
   Whom angels greet with anthems sweet,
   While shepherds watch are keeping?

Refrain This, this is Christ the King;
Whom shepherds guard and angels sing:
Haste, haste to bring Him laud,
The Babe, the Son of Mary.

2. So bring Him incense, gold and myrrh,
   Come peasant, king to own Him;
   The King of kings salvation brings,
   Let loving hearts enthrone Him.

Refrain Raise, raise the song on high,
The Virgin sings her lullaby:
Joy, joy, for Christ is born,
The Babe, the Son of Mary.